QUEERING THE
APOCALYPSE

poems for the end of the world

© Double Text Media and the Authors
First printing 2025
Published by Double Text Media
Long Beach, CA
www.doubletextmedia.com

ISBN: 979-8-9913662-1-2

"Our Lady of Apocalypse" was originally published by Dark Onus Press.

"When we joke about the zombie apocalypse until you promise you'll kill me if I get bit" was originally published in *The Ways I Tried to Call You Home.*

Queering the Apocalypse: Poems for the End of the World

Featuring

Adrian S Costello
Bellamy Watson
Caleb
Christina Brown
Dakota O'Hara
David Cole
Ellen Webre
Evan Chelsee
Gabriel Rosenstock
Gahl Liberzon

Josette
Julia Cheng
Larry D. Thacker
Liz Mariani
Miyin Delgado Karl
Paula Macena
Peter Stark
Sam C. Ponke
Tony Godino

Table of Contents

When the world ended

When the world ended I was at the mechanic
my car had sputtered to a modest stop, driving east
on highway twenty-four.

I gave the man in coveralls my keys and walked home
through a stretch of neighborhood I'd never seen.
I did not notice the erratic flight of birds over my head,
or the emptying streets.

When ash started raining down a few cities over
I was getting high in my bedroom.
I thought nothing of the crazed clanging of churchbells,
or instructions being read through a megaphone
too far away to understand.

Lindsay walked around the blocks of street barricaded shut:
a maze of faceless cops and abandoned cars
with their turn signals still blinking.

She climbed into my bed and we slept for a while
with my chin on top of her head and her hair tickling my nose all night.
In the morning she'd put on her shoes and drive home to Pasadena,
a city that I can no longer imagine.

As for me, I think I'll lay here while I can,
under my grandmother's ramshackle quilt,
and wait until my apartment building crumbles
back into the street

January 5, 2024
Berkeley, CA

—*Josette*

Our Lady of Apocalypse

Starting with a line by Traci Brimhall

Imagine half the world ends and half the world continues,
bathed in flames. A country made wretched by heretics

who root the soil, whose ashes have inked black the eyelids
of a fatal woman. I have tasted at the earth beneath her heels,

as if the berries she has crushed beneath them were libation
for a starving god. She moves like a trail of smoke, she listens

with a body that is a door to exile. Tell me, pilgrim, that her hands
are condemned animals. Tell me her smile is an open grave

so I will not slice her song across the throat of every sailor
dredged on the beach. Imagine I do this, instead of bringing her

the dead men with blistered skins and maps tattooed upon them.
Imagine I do not watch her feed. Do not grow jealous

of their salvation. I have a fugitive heart. I live. I trespass.
Obedient to all that is raw and wailing. You seek absolution,

knock-kneed and penitent. As if she would choose to save you.
Hold your prayers. Can't you see it? Heaven is already here.

—*Ellen Webre*

Family Friendly Fallout

Inspired by Emily Brock's The Counterman–Diner

Glass bones and apple pie
Newspapers used to keep molotov's alight.
The coffee pot burns.
The waitress doesn't flinch

But there's chrome
Gleaming in her eyes.

There's world outside that swinging glass door– going nuclear.

When the radio static plays and die s o u t–
　　　when the siren w a i l s and somehow
　　　　　　　　　　　　　breaks the d o p p l e r
　　　　　　　　　　　　　effect

when yet another

　　　great
　　　　　big
　　　　　　　mushroom cloud
　　　　　　　lights up the sky

　　　　　　　　　　　　at least it will look
　　　　　　　　　　　　picturesque against
　　　　　　　　　　　　the neon
O P E N sign.

−*Sam C. Ponke*

When the world ends this time,

you know what to do.
You hoard the worst of your abilities and store them
where the sun don't shine; you try not to feel aghast
at the possibilities, try not to think that
something must've flipped upside down along the way.
When the world ends this time, your mom tells you
nothing will happen. Calls you a doomsdayer,
your dad tells you to love people anyway,
but the dead know nothing, speak nothing—
so if your murderer spits on your grave, where will
the love go now?
When the world ends this time, your friend calls you
and asks you to come over. She is a plane ride away and
you crave the comfort of her couch, the smell of weed in her car.
You want to watch her kiss girls on the dance floor
in the only act of rebellion you know you have,
that you are clinging to like a sinking ship.
When the world ends this time,
a group of boys play soccer in a gas station parking lot
while smoking cigarettes. They kick it into the street and
run into traffic and you wonder if they think of home. You
wonder if they write poetry in their heads, wonder if there's
anything your mind won't insist on turning into poetry.
When the world ends this time,
there will be no survivors to hear your confessions
this time around. You know this. But, look, some things
still need tending. The flowers in your vase are
wilting, so, look, there are still
things to do.
When the world ends this time,
you fly across the country into your friend's bed
and you don't hold her hand, but you kiss her good night.
You kiss her good night.

—*Paula Macena*

1/10/25

i keep coughing.

either the smoke has suffused my lungs,
or it has subdued my soul.

i do not know which
and i do not think it makes a difference.

—*Dakota O'Hara*

Half of Me Is This Horn

She sat on the toilet doin' her toenails,
oiled up and exfoliated. I came in and
told her I saw a seagull drinking from
a coolant leak on the street where a
parked car used to be. She said did it
seem okay. I think so, it was dark. It
gets dark so soon now. She said, it's
the end of the summer, not the end of
the world. I was gonna say I thought

maybe you could save me. But she
told me would you move left a little,
you're standing in my light. I went

outside, lit a cigarette, watched it all
fall down, the sun and things. I blew
smoke into the blue glow hanging over
me, listened to my neighbor's radio,
kids playing. I don't want to alarm

you, but I think I'm gonna die soon and
I don't think I can do that without you.

— Tony Godino

Thoughts Beside the Nature Preserve Parking Lot

I sit here
In the gray
Trying to hear the birds over the cars passing by

And I wonder
Where can I go
Where it isn't gray
Where the helicopter doesn't whir overhead

Where are the birds?
I would go to them
But I am stuck here, wingless, alone, unable to sing

I will go back to my car
To the noise
To nodding my head when I want to scream

The world is a cage
And I am not
Strong enough
To break
Free

—Bellamy Watson

dec 2 2020 18:26 pst

caution in the exhaustion
you can't crawl over a river like that
this is the kind of river you can die in
you have one choice
live as if you're definitely
most certainly
inconsequentially going to die
there is no swimming
in a world filling
with water
with grief
call it a drowning
call it a rising tide
either way
your lungs
fill with fluid
your heart stops

—*Liz Mariani*

Something is coming and I don't know what.

I remember my grandfather speaking quietly
about what life was like after The War.
> *"Young men would pick up their lives*
> *and plop down somewhere else*
> *just because it felt like an adventure."*
I always wondered why he whispered
through stories of prosperity.

It was because when he was a child,
there was a day that lives in infamy.
To be so young and come out of Depression
only to see the world wage war
had to have felt like a crushing weight
on shoulders not ready to carry the burden.

He whispered because those days
came at such a cost.
The flow of these good times
birthed from a delta of blood and bone.
> *"Kentucky boys have always been good*
> *at seeing the bigger picture."*

"Something is coming and I don't know what."
I whisper the words alone in the dark
because I remember the look on his face
when he talked of what had come before.

If I am lucky, then when it is done,
I will whisper about good fortune found
after all this tumult, this deceit, this fear.

But whisper is all I will be able to manage,
to not disturb the spirits of those stronger still
who did not live to see our own grandchildren.

—*David Cole*

The Breaking

what happens in the breaking
is we all fall down
caches to ashes
rust to dust

unfold our progress
like so many paper swans
make rocks instead

remember
we will be here again
remember here

how we got —
how we broke —
how we didn't —
all the alarm bells

—*Evan Chelsee*

Star-Spangled

Our boys have gone
all gone away to the stars
a long, long way from home!
Sometimes they look down
struck dumb
searching for familiar sights
apple pie
familiar sounds
mother's voice
or in search of scarred battlefields where they fought, blindly,
row after row of crosses now

Our boys have gone
Gone away to the stars

—Gabriel Rosenstock

Love Bites

Brains...
the catcall's always the same cry,
endless: *Brains...*
except this time, it's mine

the catcall's always the same cry,
comes from bone, from husk
except this time, it's mine
the gift in the bite

comes from bone, from husk
desiccating *I'm sorry* into *don't leave*
the gift in the bite
a slow rotting love

desiccating *I'm sorry* into *don't leave*
my pistol pressed to his forehead,
a slow rotting love,
his lips and teeth off my arm

my pistol pressed to his forehead
Maggie said never go out at night
his lips and teeth off my arm
I just wanted to surprise her

Maggie said never go out at night
but it was her birthday,
I just wanted to surprise her,
to get her some gardenias, something dangerous

but it was her birthday,
she who is the last and all, the least I could do,
to get her some gardenias, something dangerous
something really worth risking for

she who is the last and all, the least I could do,
treasure hunt, see the locket on that body,
something really worth risking for
so I reach forward

treasure hunt, see the locket on that body,
every body with its own wants, treasures
so I reach forward
and he bites

every body with its own wants, treasures
I'm armed
and he bites
and I undo his forehead

I'm armed
I feel the shudder between my fingers
and I undo his forehead
but it's too late

I feel the shudder between my fingers
see if I can say no to hunger blindness,
but it's too late
clip's empty

see if I can say no to hunger blindness,
the skipping record of thought,
the clip's empty
I need something to fill it,

the skipping record of thought,
my stomach's getting angry
I need something to fill it,
something with hopes

my stomach's getting angry
chewing over what aint there
something with hopes
can't find them

chewing over what aint there:
endless. Brains….
Can't find them…
Brains…

—*Gahl Liberzon*

Apocalyptic Buffet

A regular Tuesday late afternoon
after work at the Chinese buffet
and I look up, noticing a strange
and sudden quiet finding no one
there with me. I am completely
alone, the sound of my chopsticks
the loudest noise in the place.
The kitchen has fallen silent.
The waitress is on a smoke break,
I figure. The only hint that the world
hasn't ended and everything crashed
to a halt, that I'm not the last man
on earth, are the lights left on
and a little bit of steam lifting
from the food trays. I don't know
what's happened out in the world.
The sun could be down already
for all I know. I control my little rush
of panic and quiz myself, as I often do
when the thought of utter aloneness
sneaks into my mind, taking stock
of what useful items remain
around me. What about this food?
What can I salvage? How much
should I cram into my belly now?
How to transport Mongolian Beef
in my pockets. What's happened
in the mall? Where has everyone
gone? A crash of metal bowls
startles me. Hot grease sizzles

from the kitchen, snapping me
from my daydream. The waitress
approaches and sets my ticket
down along with an obligatory
fortune cookie. I hesitate, anticipating
some declaration of finality inside,
some verification of my stranded plight.
"You will soon be involved in many
gatherings and parties," it portends.
How is this a fortune, I wonder.
I leave confused and disappointed.

—*Larry D. Thacker*

Killing a god

I killed a god today.
Tomorrow it will still be remembered
And the day after worshipped again.
A week will reveal decay
And people will recognize lifeless eyes
And prayers unanswered.
A month now
And desecration begins
As people climb mighty limbs just as human as them.
They will walk and gawk,
Share photos and dance,
And laugh into dead eyes humbled with their mortal.
In the second month
They'll call the clean-ups
To rid me of my mess and discard of my trophy.
Half the year has gone
And with it that body is a half.
The unhoused have gathered to make homes not for worship.
A year and the smell is gone now.
I found femur just down the road being used
As the foundation for a tree house.
A year and I go to the site,
Watch where flowers bloom and mushrooms thrive on tender soil
The god gave life.
Animals gather at the spine sunken
From rain and buried by wind
And they live; they live.
Where do gods go when they die?
For if they created heavens and hells
Can they not create a place for each other?
I sit on the skull where once housed a mind.
I wonder should I have asked,
Would the god reply?
Was this the god my family worshipped?
Is there another?
Did the god have a family?

But I had anger,
And it was a god,
So I obfuscated blame onto metaphysical being with bones.
A decade and they've forgotten.
A grave tended by solely me the murderer
I clean moss and tend the new acorn tree.
When I near the end of this life,
As it was thought that only mortal things once do,
There may be no other to talk of this god and it will become forgotten.
But the forgetfulness of the human
Is nothing in the memory of Earth,
Swallowing god and human and animal and plant.
Half a century, the acorn drops acorns in spring,
Skull and spine are swallowed in Earth as I soon will be;
I lie on my deathbed.
A god's blood never washes from your hands.
I once grew sad seeing it
Thinking I might have killed something good.
But every thing has changed in the way that things change.
Killing deity did not kill this world
And despite my anger the world has continued.
I am human.
Killing deity did not kill this world
And despite my anger the world has continued.
I am human.
And I am dying as all things do, even gods;
And I am learning to take happiness when it comes.
A century has passed as have I.
The acorn tree is healthy and the animals are happy
And life continues; life continues.
I was human.
I killed a god.
And life is still life.

—Caleb

In These Days

We pick at the blue veins snaking
                our wrists, our breasts,
        as dark a river as any oil in the earth.

                        We dig to find
                what our heartbeats know
                        to be true,
                grow heavy-breathed,
        smearing red dust
         upon our thighs
        to bury the landing
                place

                where unwanted
        sons and daughters
                may be delivered,

                should the ground break
        beneath our feet
                and leave us
        senseless
                from our obedience
                        to the law.

We gather at the river,
        wringing our clothes
                        in our hands,
                backs bent like oxen
                        over what will rip

at the seams
when our bellies bloat.
When we wax round like pomegranates
before the bursting.

Before we vanish
into syllables of blood
and poppies,

and become
what we want to forget.

—*Ellen Webre*

Apocalypse is only ever personal

No world ever ends —

the truth is we
can't stand this
so we elect
devils in disguise
bloom bombs out of
blocks and bullets and air
stand on the neck
of the rest of the
Earth so we forget
so we feel invincible
for a millisecond
so we can pretend
to be the authors of
the universe and our
birth the beginning
of the Milky Way

the truth is we
will not see
the end

the tale will write itself
the bloody soil will blossom
and the survivors will sing
songs about the horrors
we will not get to hear

we were born in media res
like every other fucker out there
so when the world ends
the only trumpets
will be our rasping breaths

—Miyin Delgado Karl

Apocalypse Always

We had to walk down
sugar sand swamp roads
to reach him
Our way blocked by
a city garbage truck sunk in a sink hole

His name was Marty Moyte
And he made the apocalypse seem so... sexy?
He greeted us outside shirtless
His sweat pants tucked into cowboy boots
His home
pieces of plywood
pieced together
to create a windowless space
that creaked with each step
His wife
we were told
was asleep in an adjoining room
Where that room might be was a mystery
Back pain and pain pills
explaining her absence
He sprayed aerosol
to clear out the smoke from his cigarettes
"I know you can't smoke" he said
I grew light headed anyway
breathing the lemon scented cigarette stench

My companion, in his seat,
quickly fell asleep
in the sweltering heat
And so it was me and Marty
lamplit and sweating
Me, feeling choked in my white shirt and tie
grew listless and wondered
"Is this how I die?"

He told me he was an outlaw preacher
destined to be left behind
He had already crossed the line
made a deal with the devil

before coming unto Christ
But this was his life
riding a horse through the apocalypse
A Bible in one hand
A rifle in the other

"Two Men in a field, one is taken, one is left"
he leaned forward whispering
his face coming into the light
"Who will be there for those who are left behind?"
I didn't want to give him the satisfaction of saying "you"
So, I sat staring in suspense
"Me," he said, pointing at himself.
"I'm going to be there for those who are left behind"

I handed him the Bible he had ordered
(specifically requesting in-person delivery)
I looked over at my companion
He hadn't moved in many minutes
and I wondered if he was dead or taken
"Maybe the rapture is real," I thought
Not really part of Mormon theology
but I was open to the idea
And if this was the apocalypse, it wasn't so bad
Felt a bit like Florida before the apocalypse

Suffice to say, I was a bit disappointed
when my companion woke up
My visions of me and Marty galloping
through Hellfire
dashed

On our way back to the apartment that
the church provided for us
I tried to explain to my companion what happened
"Why didn't you wake me up?"
"I thought that you were dead"
"And you just sat there?"
"Well, I thought you might have been raptured"
"What are you talking about?"
"The apocalypse, but it was just my mistake"
We sat in silence

But I feel like maybe I've mistaken
my life for the apocalypse ever since
Or maybe
each life, from birth on
is its own apocalypse
The signs and omens appearing
in wrinkles around the eyes
Some of us will burn alone
Some of us burn together
but we all burn out eventually

Yesterday, the wind shifted
and the fire-orange hue
lifted from Los Angeles
And the sky was blue
I went outside to pick fruit
from my garden
I wiped ashes off apples
I tasted tangerines so sweet
Then I returned to the TV
And thought about the apocalypse
This time it was too real
I could not have been mistaken

I scanned the screen
for images of Marty
sweatpants tucked into cowboy boots
galloping through Hellfire
Who is going to be there
for those who are left behind?
I didn't see him
I turned off the TV
I sat in silence

—*Peter Stark*

keywords to use in case of emergency

memory becomes food
food becomes death
death becomes healing
healing becomes escape
escape becomes winter
winter skips spring becomes fall
fall becomes nuclear
nuclear becomes extended
extended becomes tech
tech becomes art
art becomes emergency
emergency becomes death
death becomes extended
extended becomes memory
memory becomes escape
escape becomes winter
winter becomes tech
tech becomes healing
healing becomes fall
fall becomes art
art becomes keywords
keywords become nuclear
nuclear becomes death

—Liz Mariani

When we joke about the zombie apocalypse until you promise you'll kill me if I get bit

what I hear
is when you think of the end of the world,
we are not bandaging each other's wounds.

I die in the first act, a tragic thread
of the backstory you'll tell
your one true post apocalyptic lover someday.
You are the main character,
and you only have one gun.

You grew up watching movies with men
who made it to the end days alone and so
when you imagine the end of the world,
I'm not there.

The difference between us
is I would never want to survive
the kind of apocalypse you love to read about.
But if I did, I would keep you alive.

I would try. I'd slide raw beef
under the locked bathroom door
to keep you with me. I'd fall in love
with the small hope
that might bring the old you back to me,
but I'd learn the new you.

The difference between us
is that even now, years after
I fell out of my hollow little love,
I don't want to live in a world
where you don't exist.

I am happy to know that somewhere,
someone else hears you laugh every day.
Somewhere, you are at the grocery store
buying turkey breasts and spinach.
The peppers in your garden are growing
and you are dreaming of some bright future,
a wife who takes your children to church on Sundays.

I know it is easier to have love for you
when I do not know you.
I know I love you alone.
I know you don't see me in every airport you pass through.
You do not think about my grocery lists.

The world has not ended, but still,
I am gone.

—*Christina Brown*

Solar Punk Spring

Dear, what's happened?
Years ago you liked to walk in the rain
Now that I want to, never again?

Disregard the smog and the screaming
Calls for justice flood our existence
As humble gardeners serenade their friends
Brewing homegrown resistance

Follow me, dear, under the canopy
Hidden beneath lush constellations
We'll scheme and dream of revelations

Listen to the songbirds cry
They whisper of bloodshed and blooms
Their stories carry across Earth's waters
Warnings of hope renewed

Liberation for all
The sheer magnitude, the glimmering future
Cause arms to fall

Our mother's tears catch us
She's healing our path
Don't sink into sorrow
Keep calm in our wrath

Walk with me in this cleansing rain
We'll fight through feelings together
Acknowledge the flowers, the light, the pain

—*Julia Cheng*

Impotence

There's magic
in the tenderness of hearts
beating steadily
together
even as the horrors
come. Magic in the warmth
of mirror neurons
firing. Billionaires can stuff
their pockets with everything,
but they can't
have this.

—*Adrian S Costello*

Alternate universe in which we do not destroy the planet

You and I sip lavender and honey
from my grandmother's teacups
and someday,
so will our daughters.

In August, we lie in the cool grass
and slice peaches for each other's tongues
with butter knives.

All of our egg yolks
are blood orange.
We cut the smokestacks
into playgrounds.

The ocean is just the right size
for every metaphor about depth
full of sharks with soft teeth

and whales that hold our toxic past,
the way a mother holds
a child's used tissue,
unfazed by our small biology.

All of the water is clean.
The sunshine is only ever
good for us.

When it is time to let the chaparral burn,
everyone in California
helps their neighbors pack
and we all go to summer camp.

When it is time to go home,
we know,
and we hold hands
the whole way back.

—*Christina Brown*

Looking Into the Devil's Face

You want to kill us
with the radiation of our rage
and terror but of course
you wouldn't know
that open hearts don't trap
the shadows in and when
I start to be consumed I find a way
to be a wave and when I break
at its conclusion I'm a bright defiant
love for all we are for how impossible
it is to make us small and how
you'll have to kill us if you want us
to recede and now we're ocean spilling
crashing well beyond our borders
you should know that there
are always more of us
that we're unstoppable
we're powered by the moon

—*Adrian S Costello*

There will still be crushes in the end times

I want to write about the way humanity endures, and how your body lighting up when someone smiles at you is involuntary and that's beautiful. How our lives and desires will be more important than ever when so much is stripped away. We need the apocalypse songs but we also need the love songs. We need beautiful things to remind us of the difference between surviving and living, to remind us what we're surviving towards, why we fight for each other, why our hearts still continue to pump and it is not a waste. There is so much waste but loving and living never are. Joy is a renewable resource but it has to be tended and cultivated and you can't be moved by beauty if you aren't also willing to be moved by pain. To be open for some of it is to be open for all of it. There will still be crushes at the end of the world because what is humanity if not the stupid swelling of love and desire and feelings when it doesn't make any sense? And really that makes perfect sense, because what would ever make more sense than each other—caring for and about and with and towards? That's it. That's the point. That's what I want to say.

—*Evan Chelsee*

My favorite part of YA Dystopia

is that somehow being straight is outlawed
and therefore the breeders get to save the earth

It's always two tributes, unnaturals, uglies —
it's always a boy and a girl

who fall in love despite the government's
best efforts to banish all serpents

— Adam and Katniss
Four and Eve —

tell me a story about a garden,
a rapture and a rib

but this time their kiss brings
order, paradise back to Eden

what about the rest of us
who were never allowed to exist

I would rather take apocalypse
than sanction straightness as salvation

if queer people must burn
then let's take the world
with us
let's turn our bodies into
fire and brimstone
until our bellybuttons
unscrew and spill
out into springs
that flood the whole
damn dance floor

we'll be the rainbow
after the storm

—Miyin Delgado Karl

About the Poets

Adrian S. Costello is a Brooklyn-based queer and trans writer who is fairly obsessed with taking photos of trees at Green-Wood Cemetery.

Bellamy Watson is a disabled, neurodivergent, genderqueer multipurpose creator, dabbling in poetry, game design, graphic design, art, and fanfiction. They spend their time reading, gaming, and watching TV, usually in his bed. She has a lot of feels about things going on in the world.

In the evocation realm of poetry that delves into themes of trauma and the profundity of Death, **Caleb** emerges as a poet whose words resonate deeply with raw emotion and introspection. Through carefully crafted verses, Caleb confronts the shadow of the past and the haunting uncertainties of morality, weaving together poignant imagery and lyrical cadence to explore the complexities of human existence. Each poem is a journey through layers of anguish and resilience, offering solace and understanding to those who traverse the labyrinth of their own experiences. Caleb's poetry is a testament to the power of art to illuminate the darkest corners of the soul and find beauty amidst the fragments of pain.

Christina Brown is a poet living in Long Beach, CA. Her work has appeared in The Los Angeles Press, A Moon of One's Own, The Sunshine Lounge, Ink & Marrow, Fight Evil with Poetry, and other venues. In her free time, you'll find her reading niche non-fiction books, trying not to kill her houseplants, and never getting over anything. She is the author of two poetry collections, Girl Teeth (innateDIVINITYpress) and The Ways I Tried to Call You Home (Double Text Media).

Dakota is a firmly transplanted New Jersey native, where there is nothing better to do than be concerned about things that do not matter. Luckily, this wonderful new world has provided Dakota with many tangible things to be concerned about and sometimes, if the words and fears are nurtured, they become poems. This is the first time Dakota has submitted work to be published!

David Cole (He/They) is a writer and multimedia artist from Appalachia. David can be found on bsky as @coledone.com and YouTube as @ColedOne.

Ellen Webre is a biracial, Taiwanese-American poet, born in Hong Kong and raised in California. She is currently acting as a social media marketing specialist and videographer for Moon Tide Press, is a co-host of Two Idiots Peddling Poetry, and was the managing editor of Spillway Magazine Issue #30. Ellen's debut book, A Burning Lake of Paper Suns, was released in October 2021 with Moon Tide Press and won a Best Indie Book Award in 2022. She can be found at @lnwebre on Instagram.

Evan Chelsee (they/them) is a cultural producer and organizer living in Long Beach, CA. They are usually casually obsessed. You can find Evan on the internet at evanchelsee.com

Gabriel Rosenstock is a bilingual poet (in Irish and English). He is also internationally known for haiku, tanka, children's literature, translation, short stories, novels, plays and criticism.

Gahl Liberzon is a(n as yet unzombified) research assistant in Long Beach, California. His fiction, essays, and poetry have appeared in Public School Poetry, Ghost City Review, and After Happy Hour Review. You can find his work at linktr.ee/gahllib Josette is a former English student at UC Berkeley and current scholar of the real world.

Julia Cheng is a climate optimist and sustainability enthusiast currently living in Colorado. She has a BA in English from CSUCI, a couple of mischievous cats, and a silly, but supportive, partner. She is learning how to live sustainably on Instagram @climatecheng

Larry D. Thacker's poetry and fiction can be found in over 200 journals and anthologies, including Spillway, Poetry South, The Lake, The American Journal of Poetry, and Valparaiso. His books include four full poetry collections, two chapbooks, as well as the folk history, Mountain Mysteries: The Mystic Traditions of Appalachia. His collections of short fiction include Working it Off in Labor County and Labor Days, Labor Nights, as well as a co-authored short story collection, Everyday, Monsters. His newest poetry collection is entitled New Red Words. His MFA in poetry and fiction is from West Virginia Wesleyan College. Visit his website at: www.larrydthacker.com

Liz Mariani's work has been published in Two Serious Ladies, Italian Trans Geographies edited by Danila Cannamela, Marzia Mauriello, and Summer Minerva via SUNY Press, The Brooklyner, Fortunates, Artvoice, Images Magazine, PoemTown Randolph, Great Lakes Review, The Waiting Room, The Buffalo News, After The Pause and Advaitam Speaks.
linktr.ee/lizmarianipoetry

Miyin Delgado Karl (she/her) is a Colombian writer and poet currently based in Southern California. She was born and raised in Bogotá to a mixed Asian-Latino family that nourished her with stories. Her work centers around themes of immigration, queerness, and Latin American folklore. Her poetry has been published in wildscape. literary journey, Santa Rabia Poetry, and welcometoplutos. Miyin currently works in film production and writes with equal measures of silliness and trauma.

Paula Macena is, above all, a writer. Besides this, she's a Brazilian-American who grew up in New Jersey and currently resides in Los Angeles. Aside from being published in Jr High the Magazine, Culturally Arts Collective, and Prometheus Unbound, her most recent poetry collection Penance of the Byronic Hero was released in June 2023. In her pursuit of providing a platform for writers, she is the founder and director of Pluto's, an organization that makes literature accessible to all. When she's not reading or writing, you can find her making coffee.

Peter Stark, originally from the desert of Southern Utah, now lives in Long Beach, California. He was raised Mormon. He is gay. He has spent his career traveling the world working with refugees and asylum seekers. He loves art and people who make art.

Sam is a librarian in the Midwest where he earned his Bachelor's in Creative Writing and Film Studies. His Master's in Library Science is from Kent State University. You can find his various writings like fiction and book reviews floating around the internet in places like Ghost Watch and Booklist alongside his regular contributions to the website Youtini.

Tony Godino has published short fiction with Isele Magazine and poetry with Midcult, Literary Hatchet, Museum of Americana and others. He is from Scranton, Pennsylvania and considers the 2022 MLS Cup to be the greatest heartbreak of his entire life. He can be found on Instagram here: @TonyGodinoDied

About Double Text Media

Double Text produces media that uses the deeply personal as a lens for engaging the world. Our work is by and about queer people, and the way they move between text and subtext.

www.doubletextmedia.com

Also from Double Text

Recurring Characters by Evan Chelsee

The Ways I Tried to Call You Home by Christina Brown

www.ingramcontent.com/pod-product-compliance
Lightning Source LLC
Chambersburg PA
CBHW051600120626
46551CB00013B/1595